pocket: *adjective*
issue: *noun:* a vit

Born from a frustra
news, Pocket Issue   ⌐ of
the biggest challeng⌐   ⌐ ιne facts in an
independent and quic

Designed for our time-μ.⌐ssed lives, these short and pithy
handbooks quickly brief you with enough facts to join the debate.

Praise for Pocket Issue:

*'A brilliant wheeze: The essence of the debate in a very
approachable format.'* Harriet Lane, The Observer

*'Exactly what any busy person needs – the facts at your fingertips!
Never get caught out again when a conversation starts on the big
issues of our time.'* Jeremy Vine, BBC Radio 2 and Panorama

*'For everyone who longs to be well-informed but lacks the time
(or attention span).'* Alex Clark, The Observer

*'Prep yourself by keeping the one on global warming in the
downstairs loo...'* Mary Killen, The Spectator

'Precisely what's needed...' Hephzibah Anderson, The Daily Mail

Sign up for news of forthcoming publications and special offers at
www.**pocket**issue.com. And tell us what you think, we always
welcome your suggestions and comments.

Pocket issue
Small briefs for a big world

1

Pocket Issue
Food

what are we really eating?

Published by Pocket Issue, London
www.**pocket***issue*.com
info@**pocket***issue*.com

Copyright © Pocket Issue, 2007

ISBN: 978-0-9554415-3-0
ISBN: 0-9554415-3-6   ·

Design and production by Sanchez Design.
www.sanchezdesign.co.uk

Pocket
ISSUE

Each Pocket issue is written to a standard editorial template. For Food – *What are we really eating?* we would like to thank the following team:

Researcher: Was Yaqoob
Author: Mary Alexander
Illustrations: Andrzej Krauze
Design: Daniel Sanchez
Editorial: Nat Price, Victoria Lane

We would also like to thank those who have offered help and advice along the way: Julia Hartley, Maria Earle, Johnny Sandelson, Joanna Everard, Julia Bullock, Nick Band, Victoria Dean, Dr Jonathan Parry and Richard Sunderland.

The Pocket Issue Team

Contents

One Minute Guide

The issues in the blink of an eye

ONE MINUTE GUIDE

Going to a 'foodie' dinner party? Need to get the facts quickly?
Gen up on the issues with our One Minute Guide to Food.

Dazzled by choice?

Not so long ago, we ate to survive and were grateful if we went
to bed with a full stomach. Now there are 38 types of milk on
sale in supermarkets and packaging is littered with words like
"GM", "Organic" and "Fairtrade". Newspapers carry food
columns, and chefs, who once stayed largely behind the scenes,
have become celebrities. How did food get so complicated?

Doing the right thing

Eating has been described as "the most political act we do on a
daily basis" as the choices we make affect our health, our
landscape, our climate and businesses, not only in the UK but
across the world.

The rise in intensive farming

The need to be self-sufficient following the two world wars saw
the introduction of new farming techniques including factory
farms, pesticides, machinery and antibiotics. Now 96% of the
UK's farms are intensively farmed, providing us with the cheap
food we enjoy today.

The reaction against intensive farming

Consumers increasingly worry about the impact of intensive
farming methods on the quality of our food and on our health, as
well as pointing to its poor record on the environment and
animal welfare.

The organic option

Organic food - grown with limited pesticides and with better animal welfare - is one of the UK's fastest growing markets. It is certainly better for the environment, though it's still being debated whether it is really better for our health.

Fairtrade?

Fairtrade schemes give developing-world farmers a fairer deal; though they often cost the consumer more. The schemes offer positive benefits for many, for example, coffee farmers in Costa Rica, though some see Fairtrade as hampering free trade and standing in the way of more radical schemes to make world trade more equal.

Tell me more about subsidies. Don't they already hamper free trade?

Yes. The US and European governments protect their farmers through subsidies. These skew world trade and harm farmers in the developing world. Though without them, rural life may fundamentally change.

What is there to say about food and the environment?

Worldwide, more greenhouse gases - thought responsible for global warming - are released through agriculture than through flying and road transport combined. Organic farming uses half the energy of conventional, intensive farming.

'Food miles', which refers to the distance food travels from point of source to point of sale, are also bad for the environment. How food is packaged likewise has an environmental impact.

Where we buy food also has an impact.
So where is the best place to shop?

There's **no perfect answer** to this question. It all boils down to your individual priorities. For example, supermarkets provide cheap and varied food but some squeeze farmers and put profits before the environment and the community.

Food may also be heavily packaged and have clocked up a lot of food miles. Instead, you could buy 'local' food - from the high street and other outlets such as farmers' markets - which brings you closer to the producer, keeps money in the community, is often less wastefully packaged, and cuts down on food miles. However, bigger retailers may be selling 'local' food under false pretences.

ESPRESSO

So, the coffee is being passed around the table, your host is looking serene. Here are some things you should (and shouldn't say) to keep your place at the table.

Have a second helping

"I used to love fried chicken. But then you see what happens to the birds …"

"We get a lovely box of organic veg delivered. I don't know why they have to put in so many beetroots."

"I do always try to ask my butcher where his meat is from - you need to be careful these days. However, he's a bit scary. He's got some very sharp knives..."

"I don't know what to do. Do I spend my money supporting my local community? Or help parts of the world that are much poorer?"

"It's difficult to talk about organic food without sounding smug."

Get your coat

"There's nothing new about GM food. Farmers have been mixing breeds for years."

"You didn't peel the carrots? Are you trying to poison me?"

"Organic food is a con. After all, everything is organic, we're all made of carbon aren't we?"

"Fairtrade? I'm more of a Gold Blend man myself.

"Why can't I be fat? I'm not hurting anybody but myself. Anyway, you can get liposuction on the NHS now."

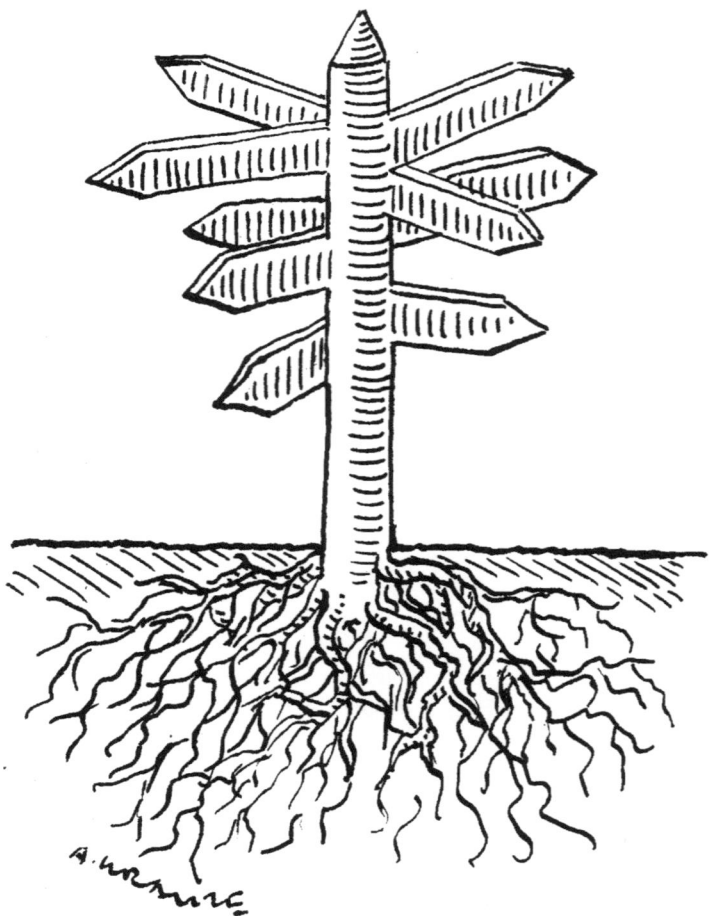

Roots

The important questions answered

THE ROOTS

Thirty years ago we were probably at the high point for food enjoyment. War rationing was behind us and food was widely available, yet food awareness hadn't really taken hold. We ate what we were given and shopped where we liked. Children were allowed to consume sweets and fizzy drinks without their parents attracting glares from the food police. The concept of 'food guilt' had not arrived.

The end of ignorance

Today, every thinking mother knows her children's lunch box should not be full of Mars bars and crisps, but brown-bread hummus sandwiches and cucumber sticks. Tea should not be a shop-bought pizza but a homemade, possibly organically sourced, nutritionally well-balanced meal. We've never led busier lives, with jobs, children and houses to run, but we are now often told that convenience meals, designed to help plug that time gap, are full of additives and high in salt and sugar. Even the quality of school dinners is under attack.

Much to do with food is now steeped in conflicting fact and myth. Only one thing is clear: with obesity levels spiralling and the government offering lessons on how to eat fruit, our relationship with food has clearly run out of control.

The healthy option

It may be tempting to think that ignorance was bliss back in the 1970s, but with life expectancy longer today than ever before (although the rising levels of obesity threaten to reverse this for the first time in 200 years), and doctors regularly declaring a number of illnesses entirely preventable if we only changed our diet, it must be worth knowing the facts about food.

As Hippocrates said, "let food be your medicine". But with so much out there on the subject, how do we begin to make sense of the issues?

Food production
The way food is produced is a key issue that should influence our daily choices. Do we accept intensively farmed food or should we switch to organic? Where do we stand on genetically modified food? Do we care about Fairtrade or food miles? Our choices have nutritional, environmental, community and political consequences.

A BRIEF HISTORY –
SUBSIDIES AND THE RISE OF ORGANICS

Once farming was about growing crops and grazing cattle. But over the course of the 20th century it became about pesticides and factory farms, subsidies and butter mountains. Pocket Issue asks how and why this happened and charts how it has affected the world.

THE RISE OF INTENSIVE FARMING

When did intensive farming start?

Today intensive farming - using technology and science to get the best returns from the land - is the dominant farming force in the Western world.

This type of farming has its roots in the early 20th century, although greater demand for cheap food has been constantly increasing since the industrial revolution in the 19th century and the dramatic rise in population.

How did it manage to dominate global farming practice?

The early 20th century brought fundamental and technological changes to age-old farming methods. These included the discovery of vitamins and their role in animal nutrition, which allowed livestock to be raised indoors by the 1920s. Antibiotics and vaccines enabled raising livestock in larger numbers and in more confined spaces through suppression of disease and the introduction of chemicals such as DDT, weed killers and ever-better fertilisers.

Did our two World Wars play a part?

UK farming became increasingly industrialised after World War I, when self-sufficiency became a key goal. In 1914, Britain was producing 30% of its own food, but by 1945 this had risen to 80%.

World War II saw the disappearance from our shops

18

of virtually all luxury food items in order to support the war effort. Rationing was introduced in Britain, with each person limited to set amounts of basic foods such as meat, cheese and sugar. Rationing continued for some time after the war, with bread and potatoes rationed at times until 1948, and meat rationed until 1954. Rationing served as a further spur to produce more, a goal supported by legislation.

96% of UK farming is intensive

What was the landmark legislation?

The UK passed two high-profile Agriculture Acts, in 1947 and 1967. These granted subsidies to farmers to encourage greater output through the introduction of new technology intensifying animal production.

Does intensive farming still dominate in the UK?

Yes. The government recently stated that 96% of UK farming is intensive. Over 70% of the UK's land is under agricultural use.

High profile health scares have been linked to intensive practices

THE FALL OF INTENSIVE FARMING

Why has there been a reaction against intensive farming?

Major concerns about animal welfare and its effects on the environment have been one driving force. Maybe more importantly, there has been a growing public perception that intensive farming poses a health risk. High-profile health scares - for example "mad cow" disease and bird flu - have been linked to intensive practices.

What are the alternatives?

Organic farming - farming with limited pesticides and better animal welfare - has grown in popularity. At first considered the preserve of sandal-wearing tree huggers, sales of organic food have grown ten-fold in the

19

last decade, though still making up only 2% of total UK grocery sales. The Archers, BBC Radio 4's everyday story of farming folk, introduced its first organic farm as far back as 1985.

GM farming has also grown in popularity, though still banned in the UK and Europe. It is very much in the mainstream in the US and is persistently knocking on our door.

SUBSIDIES – THE CASE FOR AND AGAINST

When did we start to subsidise our farmers?

After 1945, when our need to become self-sufficient drove government policy.

What is the key date?

1973 brought an end to self-sufficiency as the UK joined the European Community, making British agriculture subject to the Common Agricultural Policy (CAP). Through it, the UK exchanged national protection of agriculture for Europe-wide protection against the outside world.

What is the CAP?

CAP was created to stabilise markets, to maintain the farming community, and to ensure fairness to labour.

> Subsidies encouraged over-production, famously producing beef and butter mountains in the 1980s

A system of European agricultural subsidies and programmes that attempt to guarantee a minimum price to European farmers, it accounts for a staggering 44% of the EU's total budget in 2007.

Was the CAP responsible for the butter mountains?

Yes. The subsidies encouraged over-production, famously resulting in the beef and butter mountains in the 1980s.

Do our subsidies in the developed world hurt developing farmers?

Yes. Developing world farmers

have been hurt by schemes such as CAP because they would otherwise be able to undercut EU farmers' prices and compete more effectively. Moreover, subsidies encourage farmers in the West to over-produce and "dump" additional produce into developing world markets.

Is there an argument for subsidies?

Farmers are not just businessmen but also custodians of the land. Removing financial support could result in changes to the rural life and landscape that we know and love. Given recent concerns about global warming, this "custodian" role has gained greater importance.

Is Europe alone in subsidising its farmers?

No. The USA also has a comprehensive programme of subsidies in place. However, some developed countries, including Canada and Australia, are calling for world trade to be fairer. One estimate states that a 10% increase in access

to US sugar markets for Caribbean producers would do more to raise incomes there than all the development assistance over the past three decades.

In the UK, CAP is being replaced with a Single Payment Scheme.

Introduced in the UK in 2005 in response to EU legislation and pressure from around the world, this aims to separate payments from production. Grants are now dependent on the amount of land maintained in cultivation, and the degree of environmental friendliness.

FARMING IN THE DEVELOPING WORLD

What is the state of farming in the developing world?

Agriculture in developing nations has undergone a transformation over the past 40 years, leading to significant increases in agricultural productivity. Often termed the "Green Revolution", this was achieved mainly through the availability

21

of technologies, such as pesticides, synthetic fertilisers and irrigation methods, as well as high yielding varieties of seeds especially maize, wheat and rice.

What were the results?

Cereal production more than doubled in developing nations between 1961 and 1985. As a result the average person in the developing world now consumes about 25% more calories per day than before the Green Revolution

Do developing world farmers get a better deal from the Western world?

Subsidies continue to prevent them competing with our farmers. Retailers, such as the big supermarkets, often look overseas for cheaper produce and squeeze the margins of the developing world farmers.

Initiatives, the most notable being the Fairtrade movement, have grown in popularity as understanding of the plight of these farmers has grown.

However, new challenges are on the horizon. The link between food miles and global warming means that some consumers are now turning their back on food from the developing world.

A BRIEF HISTORY – THE ISSUES

Intensive farming responded to the growing number of mouths to feed.

Two world wars meant self-sufficiency in food production became an issue of national security for the UK.

Some Western governments have protected their farmers through legislation and subsidies to encourage intensive farming.

Subsidies have had a wide-ranging impact, distorting the market place and impacting adversely on developing world farmers.

Farming's "custodial" role has become more important.

MAKING FOOD – THE OPTIONS FOR FOOD PRODUCTION

The world of farming - how we make our food - has changed dramatically over the last century. But what do factors such as intensive farming, organic farming, GM, Fairtrade mean to us as we sit around the kitchen table? Pocket Issue takes a look.

INTENSIVE FARMING

What are the benefits of intensive farming?

It gives farmers greater control over the vagaries of Mother Nature, historically allowing them greater yields than traditional farming practices. It has also provided us, the consumers, with greater choice at cheaper prices.

Why is intensive farming criticised?

Intensive farming practices are accused of harming the environment, creating health risks and mistreating animals. However, it should be noted that the description "intensive" can cover a range of activities. For every "factory farm", where animals are regarded as little more than economic units, there are many farmers in the UK who look to use the technology available with responsibility.

Who regulates intensive farming practices?

The Department for Environment, Food and Rural Affairs (DEFRA) regulates the farming industry, and ensures that animal welfare regulations and pesticide use, as laid down by both the UK and the EU, are adhered to. Many of the worst practices are now banned in the UK and Europe - for example DDT in 1984 - due to their environmental and health impacts.

Agriculture is an important source of the greenhouse gases thought to be causing global warming

23

THE ENVIRONMENT

Does farming have an impact on global warming?

Agriculture is an important source of the greenhouse gases which are thought to be causing global warming, greater than air and road transport combined.

Sources of the world's GHGs today
Units: Gigatonnes of carbon (equivalent)

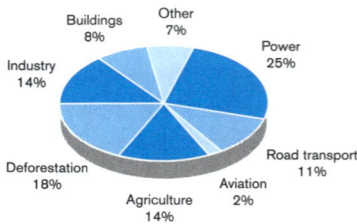

Source: Stern Report 2006

Intensive farming - with nitrogen fertilisers, greater density of animals and farm machinery to the fore - is a major driver behind this.

How does intensive farming harm the environment?

Fertilisers, pesticides and herbicides have an environmental impact. Pollution of the water table by agricultural chemicals and wastes is a major issue in almost all developed countries, and in many developing countries. Pollution from fertilisers occurs when they are applied more heavily than the crop can absorb, leaving the excess to leach into groundwater or be washed into waterways. Pesticides also damage biodiversity by destroying weeds and insects outside farmed land, removing food for other animals.

What about factory farmed animals?

Rearing animals in cages and factory-like buildings creates more disease, greenhouse gases and pollutants than traditional and organic methods of animal rearing. The concentration of many animals in a small space leads to an overflow of animal waste, to which chemicals and water have to be applied, which in turn leads to chemicals leaching into the soil.

And fish farms?

Claims have been made that fish-farming, the most recent

> **Scottish salmon farms are thought to discharge the same amount of waste as 9 million people**

development in intensive farming, helps the environment by taking the pressure off dwindling fish populations elsewhere. However, fish-farming means vast amounts of fish faeces and food waste being regularly discharged untreated into the sea. For example, Scottish salmon farms are thought to discharge the same amount of waste as 9 million people.

And, with farmed fish fed on fish pellets, energy is needed to supply feed for the fish, whereas in the wild the fish would fend for themselves. One study of Canadian farmed salmon found that for every kilo of fish produced, 2.5 litres to 5 litres of diesel fuel was consumed by the vessels catching fish to provide a meal for the salmon.

HEALTH RISKS

What about the health risks?

Food crises are a key risk. Bovine Spongiform Encephalopathy, otherwise known as "mad cow" disease or BSE, was first identified in the UK in 1986. To date, it has led to the deaths of at least 160 people. It resulted from the use of particular bone meal products in cattle feed. The disease was found in cows, and crossed into human form through the consumption of infected meat. British scientists blamed factory-farming methods for the outbreak of BSE in the 1990s.

> **The use of antibiotics in the food chain could increase human resistance to them**

Other recent farming crises in the UK include foot and mouth outbreaks in 2001 and 2007 and the 2006 bird flu outbreak in East Anglia. Raising and transporting animals in close quarters gives disease the chance to spread, hence the preventative use of antibiotics. This can lead to antibiotic-resistant strains of bacteria developing.

But there are other health risks, too. Pesticides and herbicides can pollute fresh water with carcinogens and other poisons that affect humans. And the use of antibiotics in the food chain could increase human resistance to them, limiting the effectiveness of some drugs in combating illnesses.

ANIMAL WELFARE

What does intensive farming mean for animals?

We might like to think of animals grazing in fields or chickens pecking up grain as they wander aimlessly around a farmyard. The reality is that most animals live their lives in crowded sheds, eating grain rather than grass from pasture. Intensive farming places great physiological strain on dairy cows, which are kept indoors in crowded zero-grazing

conditions, with the heifers often separated from their calves.

Hens have 550 sq cm of space, less than a sheet of A4 paper

Likewise, most hens born and raised on factory farms are crammed into cages, never stretch their wings, and never walk. In these conditions they can be aggressive to other chickens, so they have their beaks cut off when they are born. Cages are in long rows, often stacked four tiers high. Artificial lighting is used to mimic the longest days of summer to induce hens to lay the maximum number of eggs. Regulations require that hens have 550 sq cm of space, more than in the US, but less than a sheet of A4 paper. Big production lines can kill 9000 birds an hour.

Turkeys don't fare much better. Indoor rearing involves dark conditions to reduce aggressiveness, but that makes many turkeys go blind. Selective breeding can also make the birds so top-heavy that many develop leg problems and dislocated hips.

Cattle farmed intensively are fed corn kernels, together with daily antibiotic dosages to enable them to survive on their diet. Cows have a digestive system evolved to break down grass. Without the amount of roughage derived from pasture grazing, they bloat, can suffocate and develop liver abscesses.

Pigs. Over 70% of pigs in the UK are reared in intensive conditions. Factory farmed pigs are bred to put on as much lean weight as quickly as possible through the use of antibiotics. This leads to them being virtually fat-free. Breeding sows are kept indoors in sow stalls for most of their adult lives, and denied opportunities for exercise and interaction. The use of sow stalls is widespread in some countries, for example the US, Canada and Denmark. Sow stalls are now being banned in some countries including the UK and some US states. An EU wide ban comes into force in 2013.

Sheep farming is generally not intensive with sheep requiring land to graze and ruminate.

Fish. In 1970, fish-farming contributed just 3% of the world's seafood. Now a third of the world's seafood is farmed, in Norway, Britain, Iceland, Chile, China, Japan, Canada and the US. Intensive methods produce the same problems as with intensive livestock rearing. Chemicals, antibiotics and disinfectants could be contaminating fish with toxins and could cause illnesses. Cages or nets 200 foot long and 40 foot deep are stocked with up to 50,000,

Some of the less savoury aspects of factory farming are relocating to developing countries

30-inch salmon, with each fish having the equivalent of a bathtub of water.

Is intensive farming growing outside Europe?

Yes. Most importantly, as environmental, animal welfare and labour law becomes more stringent in developed countries, some of the less savoury aspects of factory farming are relocating to developing countries with more relaxed regulation.

But intensive farming practices are growing because there is a need to feed the increasing population. In some places, such as North Africa and South Asia, most of the land suitable for cultivation is already being cultivated, so the only source of production growth is through improved management and technology.

Do we need intensive farming to feed everybody in the world?

Some scientists argue that the only sustainable way to produce food is to stop using pesticides and to adopt a cautious stance towards GM food. However others argue that only intensive farming and mass production utilising pesticides, antibiotics, artificial fertilisers and GM technology can hope to feed the world's current population of 6.5 billion, let alone the more than 9 billion predicted to be alive by 2050. There is no final consensus on the matter.

INTENSIVE FARMING – THE ISSUES

Intensive farming gives the farmer greater yields and the consumer more choice and cheaper prices.

It stands accused of harming the environment, health and animal welfare.

96% of farming in the UK is still intensive.

Intensive farming is growing in the developing world.

ORGANIC FARMING

What is organic farming?

Organic farming avoids the use of synthetic or artificial fertilisers, pesticides and growth hormones, using instead crop rotation, animal manures and mechanical cultivation to maintain soil productivity. Certain processed fertilisers are allowed as is organic pest control. Maintaining the health of the soil is the cornerstone of organic farming.

How long has organic farming been around?

Organic farming grew out of a reaction to the industrialisation of agriculture in the early 20th century, but especially following the Second World War, when the use of DDT and other pesticides became increasingly widespread.

Is organic farming 'old-fashioned' farming?

Organic farming uses techniques that pre-date intensive farming, such as crop rotation, and incorporating grass, legumes and manures, rather than chemical pesticides.

> A 2001 survey in the US concluded that organic yields were 95-100% of conventional yields

But organic farming is capable of producing yields that are almost as high as conventional farms, so the connotations of "old-fashioned"- suggesting that organic farming is outdated, obsolete or otherwise unsuited to current global food requirements - are inaccurate.

A 2001 survey in the US concluded that organic yields were 95-100% of conventional yields.

Who regulates organic production in the UK?

Organic farming is the only form of agriculture in the UK that must meet legal requirements in order to qualify for the label of 'organic'. The EU sets out standards that

29

organic products must comply with. Organic food doesn't have to be completely free of chemicals, but instead of the 450 pesticides used in conventional farming, only 7 can be used in organic production.

How are farms certified organic in the UK and Europe?

In Europe: for products to be described as 'organic', the producer must hold a license from an approved certifying body that sets its standards according to European law.

In the UK: UK standards are higher than the EU's in some respects: the Soil Association, the leading body that certifies farms as organic, has higher animal-welfare standards than the minimum EU requirement.

In Europe: Each European country has a body that certifies farms as organic conforming to basic EU guidelines.

In the developing world:
Around 80% of the developing world producers may already be producing according to internationally recognised organic standards without realising it, as small-scale agriculture is still common.

There are more than 4,639 organic producers in the UK, an annual increase of 7%

How widespread is organic farming?

Organic farming currently represents less than 2% of all the farms in the UK, though the market for organic produce has grown tenfold over the last decade. There are more than 4,639 organic producers in the UK, an annual increase of 7%.

THE ENVIRONMENT

Is organic farming better for the environment?

Yes. Organic farming methods pollute the environment far less

Organic farming uses at most half of the energy needed for intensive husbandry

than conventional methods. To produce high yields, organic farming of fruits, vegetables and grains uses traditional ploughing and rotating methods on the soil instead of fertilisers and pesticides. The latter can wear out the soil and allow chemicals to run into streams and the water table, having a negative effect on biodiversity. Organic farming also relies heavily on the recycling of composts to keep soils fertile. This recycling process takes carbon from the atmosphere and deposits it back in the soil.

Organic farming is also more efficient than conventional farming, using less energy per unit of yield and also saving the energy needed to produce pesticides and fertilisers. It has been estimated that, overall,

organic farming uses, at most, half of the energy needed for intensive husbandry.

BUT

There are areas of controversy. For example, the extent to which organic farming produces less carbon dioxide (CO_2) is under question. A 23-year study in the US has concluded that if organic methods were applied in all cropland in the US, 580 billion pounds of CO_2 could be saved in the soil - four times the quantity of emissions that would be saved if fuel efficiency of all US road vehicles were doubled. However, there is still debate over how long these savings could continue, as the carbon in the soil would eventually decompose and be released into the atmosphere.

The welfare of animals is one of the key principles of organic farming

And organic cows are not necessarily better for the environment. Cows produce methane, a greenhouse gas 23 times more potent than CO2. They produce around half the world's methane emissions, and produce more when they eat high fibre foods like grass. Organic cows, pasture-reared, eat more grass than intensively farmed cattle. The Vegetarian Society uses this in its advertising as an environmental reason to become vegetarian.

ANIMAL WELFARE

Is organic better for animal welfare?

Yes. The welfare of animals is one of the key principles of organic farming. It is slower and less productive, but makes for cleaner and healthier animals. Organic farmers are allowed to confine animals, but have to give them access to the outdoors. The animals are kept in smaller groups.

What are organically reared animals fed on and how do they live?

Organically certified animals in the UK have to be given an 'appropriate' diet. This rules out many types of feed, such as animal proteins - the cause of the BSE crisis - and GM food.

Cows: at least 60% of their diet must consist of fodder, roughage or silage. Organically grown feedstuffs are a necessity. Organic cows are fed on clover-rich grass, and must be allowed to graze fresh forage. Organic farmers tend to rear their beef cattle as herds and family groups, allowing them to follow their natural herding instincts, so reducing stress. Cows and calves graze pasture for most of their life.

Sheep: Organically grown foodstuffs must form the basis of the diet. Organic sheep are fed a minimum of 60% forage and a maximum of 40% concentrate feeds.

Pigs: Pigs are natural foragers. Organic pigs must be kept in free-range systems with vegetation under-foot or forage provided. Like cows, organic

32

pigs are fed mainly on clover-rich grass. Organic farms give sows straw and earth nests, much as they would build naturally, and many keep pigs together in family groups.

Poultry: Birds are allowed to eat grass, peck at insects, lay their eggs in nest boxes, and spend daylight hours outside. They are stocked in low densities, preventing aggressive behaviour and feather pecking.

Are organic animals fed organic feed?
Although ideally animal feed should be 100% organic, it is currently permissible for a percentage - a maximum of 5% for cows and sheep annually, and 15% for pigs - to not be organic. This is because present levels of production for organic feed do not produce enough material to meet demand from organic farmers.

Are organically reared animals allowed antibiotics?
Yes, but only when the animal's welfare or health is at risk.

Furthermore, to prevent this being used as a loophole, while on antibiotics, and for a period afterwards, the animal's product cannot be sold as organic.

ORGANIC FOOD AND HUMAN HEALTH

Is organic food better for human health?
This is still the subject of much debate. For example, the Soil Association says yes, but the Food Standards Agency says no.

But consumers seem to remember incidents at least as much as scientific research. The government has said it is important to peel non-organic carrots before eating them (suggesting the level of pesticides in their skin was too great to eat). So sections of the public remain wary and increasingly vote with their feet. This is illustrated by the continuing and rising demand for organic food. For example, today some 50% of bought baby food is organic.

ORGANIC – THE PROBLEMS

Is there a downside to organic farming?

The key issue here is levels of yield. Switching from intensive farming to organic farming can result in an initial drop in yield of up to 20%. However, some of this may be recoverable through organic soil management.

There is also a labour issue. Farming without insecticides and chemical pesticides requires more labour, which can be a good thing for rural employment but pushes up the price of organic produce.

Intensive farming methods mean cheaper and more varied food, less restricted by seasons and with fewer labour inputs. Since people are now

> Organic food is, on average, nearly 70% more expensive than conventionally grown food

living longer and have healthier lives, some people say this renders the 'health' benefits of organic superfluous.

Isn't organic food just a middle-class indulgence?

One survey suggested that organic food is, on average, nearly 70% more expensive than conventionally grown food. It may be that if organic farming becomes more widespread that prices would come down, but it is likely there will always be a premium for organic that could deter many consumers on lower incomes.

ORGANIC FARMING – THE ISSUES

Organic food is better for the environment and animal welfare.

There is no definitive answer as to whether it is better for health.

Organic farmers can produce similar yields to conventional farmers but more expensively.

34

GENETICALLY MODIFIED FOOD

What is GM food?
Food containing ingredients that have had their biological characteristics modified by altering their genetic make-up. Examples include soybean and corn. Foods containing GM have been on the market since the early 1980s.

> GM often introduces completely unrelated genes

Is GM the same as selective breeding?
No. Selective breeding - a process used for thousands of years to modify crops and livestock - uses the same gene pool. GM often introduces completely unrelated genes. GM tends to focus on crops, with livestock research still in its infancy.

The general thinking on GM:
The debate on GM has become hugely polarised, with proponents arguing they provide a solution to future global food shortages, and opponents calling them "Frankenstein" foods. The US public is far more accepting of them than the UK public.

What are the potential benefits of GM?
It can make some foods last longer and can add additional vitamins and flavours to make them healthier and tastier. And by increasing productivity, GM can also increase self-sufficiency in poorer countries, preventing hunger and disease.

And the potential downside?
Opponents argue that the impact of genetic engineering on plant, animal and human health is not fully understood. One concern is damage to the environment. The inserted genes could spread to wild populations, with consequences for biodiversity. They could also contaminate the crops of organic farmers. Then there is the risk that altering the genetics of plant and animal species could increase their susceptibility to

viruses and genetic mutations. Many scientists also refute the argument for increased productivity, claiming that the world produces enough food for everyone, and that it is just the poor distribution of it that is the problem.

What is the scientific consensus on GM?

There is none. While many scientists are concerned about its potential hazards, there are just as many who argue that there is no proof that genetic modification has caused problems. They believe that if the modification processes are well controlled, its effects can be controlled by science.

Have there been any disasters?

There have been no mass poisonings or environmental disasters attributable to GM technology.

Are GM crops grown in the UK?

No. Any firm wanting to grow crops here has to go through a labyrinthine approval process -

and the Government has outlined plans to protect conventional crops even if GM crops are eventually allowed.

75% of processed foods in the US contain a GM ingredient

So where are GM crops grown?

Most are grown in the US, with Argentina, Canada, Brazil and China also active in this area. It has been estimated that 75% of processed foods in the US contain a GM ingredient.

Do consumers in the UK like GM?

Not really. Lots of food companies, including Marks & Spencer, now pledge that their foods are GM free, in response to consumer demand. Most fear possible, but as yet unknown, health risks.

Does any food in the UK contain GM ingredients?

Yes. Foods such as flour, oil or glucose, or containing soya, often contain GM ingredients. However, no fresh GM food can be bought in the UK.

Where is the EU on GM?

The European Food Safety Authority, which advises EU governments on food issues, has resisted attempts to allow GM corn into the EU.

Why doesn't the EU like GM?

Arguments put forward include the fact that with heavy subsidies and price supports, EU farmers have no need to raise productivity. And from the EU's perspective, boosted European productivity via GM foods would further reduce food prices, and therefore further increase the need for already huge subsidies.

> Boosted European productivity via GM foods would further increase the need for already huge subsidies

Should it be banned?

This isn't a viable solution. The technology is available and being actively used around the world. This will grow and develop further over time. It's one to watch.

Who regulates GM food in the UK?

The final responsibility for regulating GM crops lies with the Secretary of State for the Environment, Food and Rural Affairs (DEFRA).

GM – THE ISSUES

There are no commercial GM crops grown in the UK or Europe.

There is no evidence that GM is bad for human health.

GM can offer greater yields and more robust produce.

Many fear that the potential downsides of GM are not yet understood.

37

FAIRTRADE

What is Fairtrade?

An international trading scheme set up to help producers in the developing world get fair prices for their produce, and have reasonable working conditions and trading terms with the companies they supply.

Fairtrade ensures a higher proportion of the money you pay for a Fairtrade-certified product goes to the producers, who can then pay workers better and improve their own business.

> Most of the world's coffee is grown by 2.5 million small farmers in developing countries

When did it start?

The Fairtrade labelling movement began in the 1980s when coffee prices were falling. Most of the world's coffee is grown by 2.5 million small farmers in developing countries - so the fall in coffee prices often left these farmers with not enough income to survive.

A variety of Fairtrade labels appeared on coffee, tea and chocolate in the late 1980s in a bid to give a fair return to the growers. In 1997, groups from 17 different companies set up a Fairtrade Labelling Organisation International (FLO) to harmonise international fair trade standards for certification and labelling.

Who regulates Fairtrade?

The Fairtrade Labelling Organisations International (FLO International), a non-profit multinational organisation with 23 member organisations, regulates Fairtrade across the world.

A body called FLO-CERT created by FLO International in 2004 ensures that producers and traders comply with Fairtrade standards and that producers invest benefits received through Fairtrade in development.

What sorts of goods have been Fairtrade-certified?

There are more than 300 Fairtrade goods, including tea, coffee, chocolate, bananas, cotton, herbs, spices and flowers.

Production methods are environmentally friendly and pesticide free

What are the exact criteria for Fairtrade certification?

Producers are paid a fair price that covers their living costs and provides the potential for them to save. They also have long-term contracts. Producers and workers can join unions that can protect their rights and improve their conditions. No child labour is allowed. Production methods are environmentally friendly and pesticide-free.

That sounds like there is some overlap with the organic movement?

Yes, there is some. Fairtrade emphasises sustainability and environmental friendliness. But the focus is far more on the welfare of the producers than on the environment, so producers do not have to operate according to strict organic methods to be certified as Fairtrade.

Does Fairtrade really help poor farmers?

Yes, and this is supported by several independent studies. For example, a 2002 study found that Costa Rican coffee farmers definitely saw an improved quality of life and health due to Fairtrade returns. A 2003 Colorado State University study of Latin American Fairtrade coffee producers found that they had greater access to training and education than farmers and families growing conventional coffee.

Fairtrade can only be a stop-gap solution to the plight of developing world farmers

So is there an argument against Fairtrade?

As with many developmental efforts Fairtrade has been controversial. Some see it as a kind of subsidy from the developed to the developing world that slows free-market growth, encourages over-production and inefficiencies. Because of this it can only be a stop-gap solution to the plight of developing-world farmers.

The Left argues that Fairtrade does not prevent the involvement of corporations that lack the ethical commitment to maintain the Fairtrade ethos, and may cut corners. Some also argue that it is not radical enough, playing within the current trade system rather than redefining world trade to make it fairer for all.

Is Fairtrade produce more expensive?

Often, yes. However, this can be heightened in the consumer's eyes, since supermarkets have less flexibility to make special offers because a section of Fairtrade costs are fixed.

BIODYNAMIC AGRICULTURE

What is biodynamic agriculture?

Biodynamic agriculture brings a holistic approach to farming that excludes the use of artificial chemicals and attempts to develop an inter-relationship between plants, animals and soil. The emphasis is on a spiritual relationship between the earth and the environment, and includes both arable and animal farming.

FAIRTRADE – THE ISSUES

Fairtrade aims to cut developing-world producers a fairer deal.

Many surveys show that it does provide tangible benefits to the farmers.

Criticisms include that it skews the workings of the free market, whilst some see it as not radical enough.

A spiritual relationship between the earth and the environment

It originated in Silesia, Germany (now Poland), in 1924, with lectures by Rudolf Steiner aimed at revitalising soil conditions degraded through the use of chemical fertilisers. Fertilisation aids include powdered quartz, and special compost preparations including herbs frequently used in medicinal remedies such as stinging nettles, oak bark and dandelions.

Is it a bit like organic farming?
Opponents of biodynamic agriculture argue that equal results can be achieved through organic farming.

However, biodynamic farming has some core beliefs that organic farming does not. For example, the biodynamic system believes that planting done at certain times of the calendar can bring optimum results. Biodynamic food production is found in 33 countries and is particularly strong in Holland and Germany.

Who regulates biodynamic agriculture?
Biodynamic agriculture is run by Demeter International, an organisation composed of national Demeter organisations, which sets international production standards that have to be met for producers to be certified as biodynamic. The national organisations are responsible for certifying individual biodynamic farms. Demeter was the Greek goddess of grain.

BIODYNAMIC FOOD – THE ISSUES
Farming based on holistic principles and the spiritual relationship between earth and the environment.

The general view is that equal results for soil quality and yields can be achieved with normal organic farming.

41

HEALTH AND NUTRITION –
WHAT IS BEST FOR OUR HEALTH?

Today health is one of the biggest concerns for people in the UK, and increasingly the link is being made between the state of our health and what we eat. Whereas once the drive was for food to be cheap and plentiful, today it is about quality and choosing well.

Is it all about 5-a-day?

In part. Over the last few decades, on-going research, largely driven by the government, has been raising our awareness of the impact of what we eat, so that 67% of the UK population now know they should eat at least five portions of fruit and vegetables a day. This is up from 43% in 2000 but still leaves a third of the population unenlightened.

Is it all about buying organic?

At the same time, the number of people buying organic is increasing year on year. One in four consumers in the UK have bought organic meat or dairy

One in four consumers in the UK have bought organic meat or dairy products

products and more than half have purchased organic fruit and vegetables. Health issues as well as animal welfare concerns and increasing environmental awareness are driving change. But is organic really better for us, or will the intensively farmed option do just as well?

So is organic better for our health?

This issue remains unresolved. Some scientific studies say yes, while others say no, often depending on the source and motives of the researcher. The nutritional value of organic food versus intensively farmed food is still being heavily investigated and widely debated, with new and often conflicting reports coming out all the time. The British, French and Swedish government food

agencies have recently concluded that there is no evidence that organic food is safer or more nutritious than conventionally grown food.

Having said that, the FSA has recently stated that it will review the health benefits of organic food following the findings of a pan EU study, yet to be peer reviewed, which presents further evidence that organic produce contains significantly higher levels of vitamins and minerals.

Organic food can contain more protective antioxidants, useful in the prevention and treatment of cancer

There are also some unquantifiable elements in intensive farming. Just one example is whether the routine use of antibiotics in intensively reared animals causes greater antibiotic resistance in humans.

43

While the debate rages on, what can definitely be said about organic food?

It can contain fewer toxins such as synthetic pesticides and more protective antioxidants, often suppressed by pesticides in intensively farmed foods, many of which are useful in the prevention and treatment of cancer.

In terms of prepared foodstuffs, organic foods contain fewer food additives, as organic standards prohibit food manufacturers from using many ingredients that may be shown to be harmful to human health.

SOME RECENT STUDIES CONCLUDED

Organic **milk** is naturally higher in certain nutrients than non-organic milk. Omega 3, an essential fatty acid, is one of them. One study indicated that organic milk can contain up to 71% more Omega 3 than non-organic; another found organic milk has higher levels of vitamin E, vitamin A and antioxidants. Organic **chicken** contains 25% less fat than intensively reared chicken. A ten-year study comparing organic **tomatoes** with non-organic found that organic tomatoes have nearly double the amount of flavonoids, an antioxidant, that protect the heart.

But aren't the risks of E-coli higher for organic food?

In principle, yes, as organic food is usually grown in manure which provides a natural breeding ground for E-coli. The risk can be minimised through the careful composting of manure, an essential tenet of organic farming, which kills E-coli and other potentially harmful bacteria.

A recent government survey has given organic food a clean bill of health in this area, though there have been some high-profile "scares", such as organic mushrooms being removed from Tesco's shelves in 2000.

Are GM foods bad for your health?
The British Medical

Association's current position is that there is little evidence that GM foods are harmful to human health. Doubts still remain in the public mind.

HEALTH & PROCESSED FOODS

However, making a healthy choice is more than simply picking up the organic apples rather than the possibly pesticide-covered ones. There are other things that need considering. For example, what happens when a number of ingredients are combined into an end product?

> The world consumes US $ 3.2 trillion worth of processed foods each year

The world consumes $3.2 trillion worth of processed foods each year, but is there any such thing as a healthy ready meal? Or does this fall into the category of junk food?

What is junk food?

Junk food describes food that is perceived to be unhealthy or to have poor nutritional value. The term was apparently first used in 1972, which highlights

> Junk food is linked to obesity, heart disease and type 2 diabetes

a time when food was freely available but widespread nutritional awareness had yet to take hold. An element of snobbery can come into what is deemed to be junk food, but typically it will contain high levels of fat, salt, sugar, food additives such as monosodium glutamate (MSG). It may also lack vitamins, protein and fibre.

Why does junk food exist?

Junk food has been popular with consumers because it is convenient. It is easy to buy, being widely available in supermarkets and fast-food outlets, requires minimal or zero preparation and has lots of flavour.

45

But consumption of junk food is linked to obesity, as well as a number of other life-threatening conditions including heart disease and type 2 diabetes. Most recently, there has been a crackdown on the targeting of junk food at children, including that served up in school canteens for children's lunches.

A healthy ready meal?

The answer should be on the label. Labels are there to help us work out whether we want to buy certain processed foods, let alone eat them.

By law, food must be marked or labelled with the name of the food and a list of ingredients. This ingredients list is a good place to start, indicating additives and salt and sugar, and it's worth looking at these, as we regularly exceed recommended intakes to our detriment.

How can we tell what are the healthy limits?

There are "Guideline Daily Amounts" (GDAs) that most producers now adhere to and publish on packaging. They are a guide rather than a target as other factors such as age and exercise do play a part.

For example, the recommended amount of salt for an adult per day is 6g but on average most adults consume 9 to 10g. Doctors predict reducing to 6g could prevent 70,000 heart attacks and strokes a year.

UK Government Guideline Daily Amounts
(GDAs) for an average adult or child

	Men	Women	Children (5-10)
Calories	2500	2000	1800
Sugars	120g	90g	85g
Fat	95g	70g	70g
Saturated Fat	30g	20g	20g
Salt	6g	6g	4g

Are GDAs related to the "traffic light scheme"?

Yes. Many supermarkets have backed a "traffic light" scheme proposed by the Food Standards Agency - green for low, orange for medium and red for high - to help easily communicate the GDAs. Calories are not included at present.

What about E-numbers?

Food additives must be listed on a product either by name or E-number. An E-number means that it has been cleared as safe to use within the European Union based on the latest scientific input.

Some additives are functional - such as antioxidants to prevent food going off (usually E300s), preservatives to increase shelf-life (E200s), and emulsifiers or stabilisers to maintain texture (E400s). Other additives are decorative - colours (E100s), sweeteners (E900s) and flavour enhancers (varied).

Some E-numbers to be aware of:

There are over 300 E-numbers currently cleared for use. Some high-profile ones to keep in mind are:

Treat with caution

Some combinations of colours such as sunset yellow (E110), tartrazine (E102) or allura red (E104) have been known to adversely affect children's behaviour. Sweeteners such as saccharine (E954) or aspartame (E951) should be used with caution with young children.

Flavour-enhancer monosodium glutamate (MSG - E651) has been indirectly linked to obesity.

Not to worry about

Vitamin C (E300) is one of the most commonly used antioxidants.

Pectin (E400) has been used to help gel jam for over a century.

47

A final thought…

Many nutritionists advise that if something is not a recognisable food, it makes sense to think twice about eating it. If you wouldn't put it in your homemade version of a dish, do you want it in the shop-bought one?

HEALTH AND NUTRITION – THE ISSUES

There is no final evidence that organic is more healthy than intensively farmed food.

There are some established health benefits that go with certain organic products.

Processed foods span the grocery industry, from the basic can of own-brand baked beans to an organic version. Read the label to find the healthiest option.

We know home cooking is best, but ready meals don't have to be a disaster: new healthier ranges are coming out all the time. Again, read the label for salt, sugar and fat content as well as additives and obvious bad stuff.

INFORMATION – FOOD LABELLING AND OTHER STORIES

It's all very well knowing that you want to buy organic meat, or vegetables grown without pesticides, but how can you be sure that's what you are doing? Pocket Issue flags up some of the clues to look for.

ORGANIC

What does it mean if the product is labelled 'organic'?

If 95% or more organic ingredients are used, the product may be called organic in the title. If 70-95% of the ingredients used are organic, then the term 'organic' may only be used in the ingredients listing. If less than 70% of the ingredients are organic, then the term 'organic' may not be used anywhere on the product packaging.

So how do you recognise organic produce in the UK?

You can recognise organic produce by the use of logos from licensed accrediting bodies. These are as follows:

UK1 – DEFRA
UK2 – Organic Farmers and Growers (OF&G)

UK3 – Scottish Organic Producers Association (SOPA)
UK4 – Organic Food Federation (OFF)
UK5 – Soil Association Certification Ltd (SA Cert)
UK6 – Demeter/Biodynamic Agriculture Association (BDAA)
UK7 – Irish Organic Farmers' & Growers' Association (IOFGA)
UK8 – Food Certification (Scotland) Ltd
UK9 – Organic Trust Ltd

If you buy loose food that isn't packaged but is called 'organic', such as fruit, the shop must be able to show you proof of an organic certificate. The Soil Association is the primary organic labelling association

RED TRACTOR LABELLING

What is Red Tractor labelling?

This was launched in 2000, and provides an assurance that

49

the product has been produced according to UK standards of pesticides, GM and animal welfare. It is run by Assured Food Standards, an independent, not-for-profit organisation set up to run it involving farmers and retailers.

Why was it set up?
Because in the 1990s, the British public wanted more information about how their food was produced and handled. It now appears on £5 billion worth of food every year and accounts for 60% of own-brand fresh foods sold in UK supermarkets.

Is Red Tractor food home-grown?
Generally but not always. Shoppers need to check the flag shown by the Red Tractor to see the country of origin.

What are the pros and cons of the Red Tractor?
On the plus side, it gives shoppers some peace of mind over the product's provenance, welfare, packaging and transport standards. On the

minus side, Red Tractor has come into considerable criticism over overstating its environmental standards. Most produce is intensively grown or reared.

OTHER LABELS

What's the status on GM Information?
Producers are legally obliged to tell you whether GM ingredients are involved.

Fairtrade?
Fairtrade goods are all clearly labelled.

Vegetarian Society logo?
Guarantees that food is free of animal products, as well as free from cross-contamination between vegetarian and non-vegetarian items during production.

RSPCA Freedom Food?
Set up by the RSPCA to improve animal welfare, the label applies to meat, eggs and dairy products from animals reared, transported and slaughtered in accordance with

the RSPCA's five standards of welfare. It is generally only found in the larger supermarkets and some independent shops.

The Leaf Marque?

A relatively new consumer label. LEAF - Linking the Environment and Farming - indicates that the producer is environmentally responsible, though is not necessarily organic.

'Fish Forever' seal?

The Marine Stewardship Council, formed in 1997 by WWF and Unilever, the world's largest buyer of seafood, has used standards based on the UN Food and Agriculture Organisation Code of Conduct for responsible fisheries.

Fish that bear this label come from fisheries that have met the following criteria: enough fish in the fishery for it to be sustainable; minimal impact on surrounding environment; and management systems in place to ensure minimum damage to environment in the future.

There are many shades of grey in between 'organic' and 'intensively farmed'

THE "GREY AREA" – COMMON LABELS

We can read the labels. We know what organic is. We can avoid the worst excesses of junk food. But how do we find our way through the myriad of differently produced goods on our shelves that don't fall into obvious and clearly marked categories? There are many shades of grey in between 'organic' and 'intensively farmed', particularly with animal products. For example, a free-range chicken, while not organic, sounds ok, as do "barn-laid" eggs. But what do these terms and others really tell us about the animal's well-being?

So what about eggs?

Around 62% cent of hen eggs in the UK are produced using

51

the laying cage system. Another 4% use the **barn** system, where birds are kept in loose flocks confined within a shed. They are provided with perches, nest boxes and litter areas, but animal welfare groups have compared conditions to a "crowded football terrace".

Some 28% of eggs are **free range**, with birds kept in large sheds in flocks of up to 16,000. The birds have access to open-air, may be beak-trimmed and can have chemically treated feed. 6% of eggs are from organic birds, fed entirely organic feed, not beak-trimmed and, with access to outdoor runs.

> Broiler chickens are bred to reach slaughter weight within about 40 days

And the poor old broiler chickens?

The **conventional chicken** is the cheapest and therefore not surprisingly the worst-off in terms of animal welfare. Up to 40,000 birds are kept under artificial light in a closed shed. They are bred to reach slaughter weight within about 40 days. They are routinely vaccinated.

Chickens labelled **free range** must have access to open air runs covered with vegetation, and that their feed must contain at least 70% cereal. But they can also be given chemically treated feed and be treated with drugs. **Corn-fed** chickens are reared as free range but fed at least 50% maize, which gives the meat a golden colour.

Organic chickens have access to open air runs, are kept in smaller flocks, 100% organic feed where possible. The use of antibiotics and vaccinations are allowed only when the health of the chicken is at risk.

Oh dear - what about beef?

15-20% of beef produced in the UK comes from intensive farming systems where animals are kept in crowded sheds for most of their lives. (A ban introduced following the BSE outbreak prevents older cattle being used in the food chain.) The EU bans the use of growth or sex hormones to fatten up cattle and speed maturity and also forbids imports of American beef, which is produced using an array of hormones.

And pork?

Since the banning of sow stalls (on grounds of cruelty), the pig-farming industry has declined. This has led to British pig products being more expensive than in other countries. However, since the UK has relatively high pig-raising standards, it's not a terrible time to buy British. There are four quality assurance schemes to look out for in terms of labelling: the Assured British Pigs scheme, the Freedom Foods scheme, the Real Meat Company, and Organic. Although none of these ensures that the pig is reared outdoors.

And fish?

With world consumption of fish having more than tripled since 1960, a quarter of the world's commercially important ocean fish populations have been depleted. One of the key problems with fish is sustainability. Look for the Marine Stewardship Council's "Fish Forever" seal.

INFORMATION – THE ISSUES

The labels tell you a lot if you know what to look for.

Ones to trust include the Soil Association, RSPCA Freedom Food, and organic.

The Red Tractor label provides some peace of mind but it is not organic.

Fish Forever is the "gold label" for responsible fish production.

FOOD MILES – HOW FAR IS YOUR FOOD TRAVELING?

You know how your food has been made but do you know where it has come from? Food miles, "local" food, and "slow" food are all buzz words, but what do they mean?

What are food miles?

It is the distance food products travel between their source and arriving on your dinner table.

Why have food miles become an issue?

Food doesn't travel by itself and it is the impact that the flying, road and sea traffic has on the environment that concerns many.

Why have food miles increased?

International trade in food has quadrupled since 1961. This has allowed people in developed countries to have foods previously available only in season, all year round. Examples include strawberries, grapes and asparagus. It also may be cheaper for big retailers like supermarkets to buy food from less expensive producers abroad and fly it in than to buy from closer to home.

> Food now travels around 1500 miles from source to your plate - 50 % more than it did in 1979

Nearly half of our food is imported from abroad. And over half of our organic food in the UK is imported. So food that bears an organic label is not necessarily locally produced and environmentally friendly. On average, each item of food now travels around 1500 miles from source to your plate - 50% more than it did in 1979.

With their greater economies of scale, supermarkets are able to transport goods over long distances in their drive to buy cheap and sell cheap, thereby clocking up considerable food miles.

A British study examined a single meal, containing chicken from Thailand, carrots from Spain, runner beans from Zambia and potatoes from Italy, and clocked up a total of 24,364 miles. The same meal could have been made with ingredients that had travelled just 376 miles using seasonal vegetables and domestic ingredients (though it may have cost more!)

Closer to home?
Even domestically produced food is travelling larger distances - agricultural products now account for close to a third of domestic freight transport.

The cost of food miles.
DEFRA estimates that the direct social, environmental and economic costs of food transport come in at over £9 billion a year. The social cost of congestion is £5 billion per year, the social cost of accidents is £2 billion, and greenhouse gas emissions, air pollution, noise and infrastructure costs are a further £2 billion.

Is there a difference between types of food miles?

Yes. Air miles cost more in energy and CO2 emissions, while HGV miles cost more in terms of local environmental impacts. Air miles are the fastest growing mode of food transport.

Are supermarkets doing anything to reduce food miles?

With growing awareness of the environmental cost, supermarkets are moving to label carbon costs and food miles. In January 2007, Tesco, the UK's biggest food retailer,

> In 2006 the UK exported 14,000 tonnes of chocolate waffles and imported 15,000 tonnes

announced that it would put labels on all of the 70,000 products it sells so shoppers can compare carbon costs.

Are food miles just caused by retailers?

No, free trade agreements between countries allow companies and speculators to make money from importing and exporting foodstuffs. For example, in 2006 the UK exported 14,000 tonnes of chocolate waffles and imported 15,000 tonnes. We sent 21 tonnes of mineral water to Australia and brought 20 tonnes back. This does produce jobs but has a social and environmental cost.

Are there any complications?

Some observers argue that food produced less intensively overseas and then flown to the UK is more environmentally friendly than intensively home-grown food. One piece of research - albeit by a New Zealand university - estimated that over the life cycle of the produce, New Zealand lamb produced four times less carbon than British lamb.

Furthermore, turning away food that has been flown into the UK will affect farmers in the developing world, for example, vegetable growers in Kenya. Some view food miles as a smoke screen for the interests of European agriculture.

What is "local" food?
Recently, emphasis has been put on food being sold 'locally' to where it is produced, for food-mile reasons and because the less distance food has to travel, the fresher it is and the higher its nutritional content.

> Tomatoes are artificially ripened using ethylene gas

What are the positives to local food?
Local food tastes better. The nutritional quality of our food is eroded by long-range transport. Food is often picked before it is ripe, and ripened at the point of sale using artificial means. For example, tomatoes are often picked when they are green and hard so they can survive mechanical harvesting and long-range transport. They are

then artificially ripened using ethylene gas, which makes them less nutritious and tasty than ripe tomatoes from local farms or gardens.

Local food also stimulates the local economy by keeping money in the community.

The concept of local food is also a reaction to supermarkets dominating the organic food market. Farmers, food activists and some consumers are using it to define more narrowly ethically sound food choices - 'fresh, local, organic'.

Don't supermarkets offer 'local' food?
Yes. As usual, if consumers express sufficient interest, the supermarkets will respond. But their definition of 'local' is questionable, because they can and do buy local food, transport it to central packing depots across the country, before dispatching it back to stores that are located relatively near its original source. Clearly this kind of "local" food still has considerable black marks in

57

> There is no legal standard definition of what can be sold as 'local' produce

terms of food miles and nutritional loss.

Similarly, animals can be reared in one place, then moved to abattoirs across the country to be slaughtered, which raises questions of animal welfare as well as ecological ones.

Why is the term 'local' so open to distortion?

Because there is no legal standard definition of what can be sold as 'local' produce. So while farmers' markets might define local as a radius of 30 to 40 miles, supermarkets are free to form a very different definition.

What other criticisms are there of the "local" food movement?

That local food is more expensive; that by convincing consumers to buy local food over and above imported food, it damages developing economies which often rely on food exports.

I've heard of 'fast food' but what is "slow food"?

The slow food movement was founded by the Italian journalist Carlo Petrini to protect endangered local foods from being extinguished by global brands. Seasonality is vital. Petrini says that though it is a constraint, it is much less of one than having to 'be forced to eat standardised, tasteless industrial food products full of preservatives and artificial flavourings'.

The slow food movement has more than 80,000 members in more than 100 countries.

> The Slow Food movement has more than 80,000 members in more than 100 countries

Food miles' close cousin: packaging

Local foods are often consumed fresh. But transported food requires huge amounts of packaging, which produces waste. In the UK, at least a quarter of household waste is packaging, two-thirds of which comes from food.

For example, an aluminium can of peas uses 4.5 times as much energy for packaging than the equivalent locally sourced produce. And much packaging is non-biodegradable plastic, which ends up in dense, poorly aerated landfills, where even paper cannot break down.

Transporting food any distance requires large amounts of non-biodegradable plastic packaging.

FOOD MILES – THE ISSUES

The distance food travels has increased 50% since 1979.

Food miles post an environmental cost through carbon emissions from transport.

In some cases, imported food may be "greener" than the home-grown choice.

Buying "local" means fresher food but closes the market to many developing- world farmers.

Local food helps support the local economy, though the term is open to abuse.

Local food can reduce packaging, which makes up nearly a fifth of all household waste.

GOING SHOPPING – FROM SUPERMARKETS TO VIRTUAL FARMERS' MARKETS

So we want to pick up our basket and head off to the shops, but the next burning issue is where do we go? Whether to the supermarket or the farmers' market, buying slow food or local food, there are choices to be made.

SUPERMARKETS

In the developed world, almost all food is purchased in supermarkets. The UK supermarkets enjoy combined annual sales of £95 billion. In our rushed, time-poor society, they are usually the most convenient places to buy food, concentrating everything under one roof, and with a huge raft of enticing offers like loyalty cards, 3-for-2 deals and constantly competitive prices. Asda's recent sale of chickens for just £2 each made the headlines.

But cheapest isn't always the best, is it?

No. Offering products at such low prices has a significant downside. Often it means (as in the case of the Asda £2 chicken) that intensive farming methods are used to produce the products. Also, as happened recently, the supermarkets stand accused of using bullying tactics to ensure farmers sell them their goods at rock bottom prices, often driving them to the brink of bankruptcy. Ultimately, such pressure could result in the decline of British farming and the UK no longer having the option to be a self-sufficient country in its food supply.

> The term 'organic' has become a marketable commodity

But supermarkets also offer organic food?

Yes. As consumers become more concerned with the potential health problems caused by intensive farming and mass production, and as demand for organic products has risen, the supermarkets have become more interested. Now everyone from M&S to Sainsbury's supplies a range of organic food. The term 'organic' has become a marketable commodity.

Is this a good thing?

There are benefits. With the supermarkets' economies of scale, organic food is made more widely available to consumers at a lower cost. This also brings knock-on benefits to the environment and animal welfare.

Is there a downside to supermarket expansion into the organic sector?

The organic sector was one way for producers to differentiate their products from the food more widely available in supermarkets, retaining a greater slice of reward themselves in an industry that too often struggles to make ends meet. However, since supermarkets are driven by consumer demand, it was inevitable that as demand for

organic grew, so would the involvement of the supermarkets. The trade-off for selling more is that big business and supermarkets put pressure on smaller, local competitors, forcing organic suppliers and producers to cut prices in order to keep the supermarkets' margins high. Some also suspect that supermarkets add an unjustified premium to organic food as it is bought by less "cash-conscious" shoppers.

However, the legal enforcement of organic standards means that supermarkets, while increasing choice and lowering prices of organic foods through their immense buying power, will actually bring more money into the organic industry.

The alternatives to the supermarkets

THE HIGH STREET

The high street has been under continued pressure from supermarkets (both out-of-town and smaller in-town

61

> Supermarkets' share of the grocery market has grown from 8% in 1969 to nearly 75% today

"metro" versions).
6000 specialist shops - grocers, butchers, bakers, fishmongers amongst them - closed during the recession of the 1990s. The supermarkets' share of the grocery market has grown from 8% in 1969 to nearly 75% now.

Many high streets, however, still have a range of smaller specialist shops selling organic and local produce, as well as butchers, grocers and bakery shops. These offer an alternative to the one-stop shop of the supermarket, often have much less packaging than supermarket goods, and support your local community.

However, many high-street shops continue to sell food that has racked up significant food miles.

FARMERS' MARKETS

Farmers' markets were once common worldwide, but declined as global trade and supermarkets took hold. Recently there has been a revival as people reacquaint themselves with the benefits of fresh, locally sourced food. In 1997 there was only one farmers' market in the whole of the UK. By 2002 there were around 450.

> In 1997 there was only one farmer's market in the whole of the UK. By 2002 there were around 450

What exactly is a farmers' market?
Farmers go to towns and locations in big cities to set up stalls and sell their produce - providing fresh, cheap, often organic and local foodstuffs.

62

Do farmers' markets just sell organic food?

No. Some food may be produced using conventional methods, and some may be in the process of being certified. There have been cases of some producers passing food off as organic to unwary customers but these are generally rare.

Are farmers' markets truly local?

The National Association of Farmers' Markets (FARMA) accredit those that sell food from within a radius of 30 miles (50 miles if in a bigger city or for more specialist produce, such as cheese).

THE VIRTUAL FARMERS' MARKET

Virtual farmers' markets support local producers and enable consumers to find out where their local markets and farm shops are. Big Barn (www.bigbarn.co.uk) is one of the biggest in the UK.

"Box" schemes, whereby seasonal, usually organic, food is delivered to your door, are also growing in number.

GOING SHOPPING – THE ISSUES

Supermarkets make life easy but are relentlessly profit-driven, and tales of exploiting suppliers abound.

Supporting your local shops helps keep your community alive, but doesn't mean the food is sourced locally.

Getting nearer to the farm gate, where possible, is a good option in terms of nutrition and reducing food miles.

A. KRAUZE

The Key Players

The people and institutions that influence the food that we eat

THE KEY PLAYERS

THE PRODUCERS: FARMERS

Farmers' **incomes** in the UK are on the floor - partly due to long-term trends of increasing competition from foreign countries in beef and milk, and partly through the buying power of supermarkets, which at its most extreme means that farmers make minimal profits or even less than the production costs for their goods.

Recent **food crises** have made things much worse. The 2001 foot and mouth outbreak saw 2000 cases of disease in farms covering most of the British countryside, leading to 7 million sheep and cattle being killed to halt disease. This causes significant damage to the UK livestock industry and with recurrences of disease - such as in summer 2007 - it is difficult for farms to recover fully though compensation payments are available from the government.

Farmers face **difficult** business decisions, with the end of production-based subsidies, deemed wasteful and damaging to the developing world, and with increased emphasis on environmental performance and quality.

On the upside, DEFRA is cutting back on farmers' paperwork, which had become increasingly time-consuming and inefficient.

The main voice of the farming industry is the **National Union of Farmers (NFU)** and their Scottish and Northern Irish counterparts.

What can they do?
Invest beyond the farm gates. Rather than allowing redistributors to take such a large cut of the profits of produce, they need to find other outlets for their goods. These could include farm shops, markets, virtual outlets and home delivery schemes that enable them to reach consumers more directly.

What about switching to organic?

Part of agriculture's overall decline has to do with the 'robust' buying practices of supermarkets that keep farm profits low. With the supermarkets holding so much power, too often suppliers don't get a fair deal, making it hard for them to make a living. Switching to organic could offset this, as it offers a chance for farmers to raise their incomes by receiving higher margins for their produce.

Organic farming can have more up-front costs. It requires more labour to maintain yields, crops are grown less often in the same piece of ground, animals are held at lower stocking densities, and seeds and animal feeds cost more than non-organic versions. But organic farming saves on artificial pesticides, and expected returns, with organic food being priced at a premium, could eventually be greater.

Organic farming also means a greater investment in the local community, because being more labour-intensive, it provides more jobs.

However, the **conversion process** from intensive farming to organic farming takes two years. During this time all land must be pesticide-free, yet yields from the land cannot be marketed as organic and sold at the premium organic food benefits from. A conversion grant is payable to farmers during this time.

THE LESS-THAN-SCRUPULOUS

There are always those who bend or break the rules for their own benefit. Recently this has included a few producers applying intensive production techniques to organic foods. For example, a Sunday Times investigation found that "organic" eggs, sold at more than twice the price of conventional eggs, were being bred from chickens reared in windowless sheds and fed on non-organic soya and fishmeal. Once reared, the chickens were moved around the country to organic areas for egg-laying. Other ways of exploiting loopholes in organic regulation include buying non-organic chicks and using up to 15% non-organic feed. Obviously this doesn't help farmers or the organic industry as a whole.

THE RETAILERS: SUPERMARKETS

At present, the supermarkets hold almost three-quarters (74.4%) of the grocery market. **Tesco**, the UK's number one supermarket, has the biggest share, taking £1 of every £8 spent by consumers. This makes them one of the most powerful businesses in the UK as well as allowing them to expand their operations worldwide.

Who are they answerable to?
Most supermarkets are directly answerable to their shareholders, which means profit comes first. Some supermarkets working in the UK also have foreign

ownership, for example the US company Wal-Mart own **Asda**, whilst a Qatari company is building a substantial stake in **Sainsbury's.**

With so much power, who makes sure the supermarkets play fair?
Scrutiny on major supermarkets by watchdogs is constant. The **Competition Commission** recently found evidence that Tesco and Asda used "threatening language" in their demands to suppliers.

Are there any rules governing the relationship between retailers and suppliers?
Yes. A code of conduct covering supermarkets and suppliers was introduced in 2002, but many think it does not offer adequate protection and some suppliers fear losing their contracts if they invoke the code during their dealings with the supermarkets.

Some supermarkets - for example **Waitrose** - now put greater emphasis on the relationship with suppliers, buying British when possible.

68

What does the code do?

It bans stores from charging suppliers for the display of their goods in favourable positions and for promotions such as 'buy one, get one free'. However, some goods are not covered, such as milk, meat and bread.

SPECIALIST SHOPS

Local grocers, butchers and delicatessens are struggling to survive against the ever-growing force of the supermarkets, particularly as the supermarkets continue to move into the convenience-shop market with their "local" stores.

According to the Grocer Yearbook, eight independent shops close every day. The All-Party Parliamentary Small Shops Group report *High Street Britain: 2015,* published in February 2006, found "that many small shops across the UK will have ceased trading by 2015 with few independent businesses taking their place. Their loss, largely the result of a heavily unbalanced trading environment, will damage the UK socially, economically and environmentally."

THE AGRIBUSINESSES AND BIOTECH FIRMS

As with any group with vested interests, the food industry resists regulation by national or trans national governments.

In the US, agricultural corporations have huge political clout, supporting industrial farming. Doubts and problems with emerging GM agriculture technology developed by firms such as **Monsanto** (the world's leading multinational agricultural biotechnology corporation and the most commonly criticised agritech giant) are often countered through limited transparency, aggressive litigation and political lobbying. This is why Monsanto is so controversial and the bête noir of environmental activists and anti-globalisation campaigners worldwide.

While well regulated, GM undoubtedly offers huge potential for both increased efficiency and yields. It is not a cure-all solution, and its operation in the hands of multinationals will not necessarily improve the lot of developing-world farmers, but may, instead, put many at the mercy of large corporations, for example with the need to replace GM seed every year. (Since the 1990s, Monsanto has sued around 150 US farmers for patent infringement - arguing that farmers saving GM seed from one season to plant in the next are violating their technology agreement. This process could be transferred to the developing world, where poor farmers have far greater motives to save seed.)

THE GOVERNMENT

Alongside consumer pressure, the Government and its various food-related agencies are a main driver in the food industry, and responsible for trying to manage and support change,

and to ensure balance and fair play in the grocery business.

If food safety problems emerge, for example, E-coli in the organic sector, issues with GM food (if GM technology ever gets past the EU and national regulatory boards) or livestock problems such as foot and mouth, bird flu or blue tongue, the **Food Standards Agency (FSA)** is the first enforcer, responsible for protecting public health with relation to food.

THE INDEPENDENT ORGANISATIONS

These include bodies such as the **National Federation of Women's Institutes (NFWI)**, the **Countryside Alliance, Friends of the Earth** and the **Soil Association.** Persistent, informed voices from all of these organisations regularly raise the issue of the decline of sustainable farming in the UK amongst other things, linking it directly to the muscle-flexing supermarkets whose astonishing buying power means that they pay farmers the minimum they can get away with, sometimes even less than the cost of production.

The NFWI submitted a report to the Office of Fair Trading in 2006 stating that: "the NFWI is concerned that supermarket purchasing practices are resulting in 40 farmers and 30 farm workers in the UK being forced off the land every day".

THE INTERNATIONAL BODIES: THE WORLD TRADE ORGANISATION

The free trade rules of the **WTO** prevent countries, or groups of countries such as the EU, from banning imports on ethical or environmental grounds. For example, although the EU will ban battery cages from 2012, it cannot ban the import of battery eggs. This means it is possible that European farmers will be undercut by cheaper imported battery eggs. Which in turn means that the EU is considering reviewing and possibly dropping its ban. Clearly unsatisfactory. Reforming WTO rules to take into account animal welfare and environmental considerations in food imports would actually grant farmers in developing countries an advantage. As most already rear animals in small-scale extensive systems rather than intensive ones, they would gain a competitive advantage over industrial farming systems.

THE CONSUMERS

Consumers are increasingly concerned about **health issues.** They need ready access to affordable and healthy food. This requires them to take the initiative themselves, and not just respond passively to government attempts to improve health, such as their "5-a-day" and "healthy school lunches" campaigns. Concerns about **food safety** - E-coli, BSE, foot and mouth, bird flu, as well as about additives and hormone levels in our food have made consumers wary of intensive farming practices.

71

Although it is regularly claimed that many pesticides are harmless and that there is no nutritional benefit to eating organic food, evidence shows that many consumers remain unconvinced and are voting with their feet. For example, some 50% of bought baby food is organic.

Consumerism is the view that consumers, rather than producers, should control the way the economy works. On this basis, the food choices consumers make will ultimately shape our retail and agricultural set-ups. To date, price-led consumerism has dominated the market for food in the developed world. However, 'green' or 'ethical' consumerism is growing.

Consumer demand for ever cheaper foods regardless of environmental and social costs is a vital factor in encouraging and allowing agricultural businesses to maintain intensive farming practices. This is food at the lowest price to the consumer, regardless of hidden environmental and social costs. Different consumer choices can obviously bring about different results.

Environmental concerns, including global warming, the impact of food miles and CO_2 emissions from intensive farming are also pushing consumers to consider local food as well as organic. This often conflicts with the imperatives of organic and Fairtrade food. So, consumers are forced to balance many things:

• Affordability – which intensive farming provides better than the alternatives.

• Environmental concerns.

• Political concerns such as the need to support farmers in developing countries.

Stargazing

What would be a good and bad scenario come 2020?

STARGAZING

Until recently, consumers have taken for granted the cheap and varied food that they find in the supermarkets. But a greater understanding of the effects that this "choice" is having on health, climate and farmers across the world is beginning to foster change. Pocket Issue looks at two possible scenarios – one good, one bad – that might have unfolded by the year 2020.

THE GOOD

Organic moves from niche to mainstream:

The UK and other leading EU member nations implement agricultural policies to stimulate the organic sector, encouraging sustainable and profitable organic farming practices.

Rural communities are reinvigorated by increased employment brought by organic farming. Consumers, ever more health conscious and alert to the nutritional benefits of organically produced food, are happy because organic food is widely and relatively inexpensively available. In fact, it starts to become the norm. The word "pesticide" starts to sound old fashioned.

Animal welfare is dramatically improved, with cage sizes across the board increased, and all livestock given opportunities to express "natural" behaviour. This in turn breeds healthier animals less susceptible to diseases. The routine use of antibiotics becomes a thing of the past. Over time, this may reverse the rise of the super bug and restore antibiotics to their full "magic bullet" power.

Supermarkets commit to fair-pricing agreements with farmers and respect the many benefits of the UK remaining a largely self-sufficient food producing nation.

In the US, although intensive farming practices take a little longer to change, massive consumer demand and the health and educational initiatives of successive governments eschewing big-business ties, leads to booming demand for organic food.

On GM: A more informed public debate having been kick-started in the 2010s, the adoption of some well-tested and proven GM foods becomes accepted worldwide, even by the EU. While never gaining credence with the organic movement, and not yet accepted in the UK, in the US GM works, together with better regulation of animal welfare and intensive farming practices, to bring about a more sustainable version of intensive farming.

In the developing world: EU and US agree to remove trade subsidies. And bilateral trade agreements, which involve bullying developing-world countries into accepting cheap EU and US food produce, are also removed.

Developing world farmers, many of whom already use sustainable and organic processes, resist the lure of intensive farming practices, and are able to successfully access the developing organic market in Europe. The booming agriculture sector in developing countries fuels prosperity, urban growth and industry, and develops domestic markets for produce.

This limits the need to export produce over long distances to distant developed-world markets.

THE BAD

Organic: never quite makes it into the mainstream. It is deemed too expensive by consumers and too "niche" by the supermarkets.

Intensive farming rumbles on, with a food scare requiring the slaughter of millions of livestock occurring on average every two years. Several polls reveal that this is deemed to be an acceptable level of "food drama" to consumers. Other surveys show that consumers return to eating the meat of the animal involved in the outbreak in ever-shortening periods of time.

However, more and more farmers decide to sell up and move into a less stressful area of employment. As a result, less and less food is produced in Britain. But the few voices raised in horror against the collapse of British farming are swatted aside as "scaremongers" by the mainstream food industry, and crushed with disparaging comments like "the supermarket shelves are filled, aren't they? Is anyone going hungry?" Certainly with obesity levels spiralling out of control, it is hard to say that they are.

The supermarkets, meanwhile, continue to report "super" profits, and open new stores up and down the land. Increasing amounts of foodstuff are imported, with a corresponding growth in food miles. Eventually, food labelled "British" sells at a premium for its rarity value.

British asparagus, for example, once a feature of a British summer, becomes as rare as truffles.

GM: GM does increase yields, but most of the technological improvements go towards satisfying Western consumer preferences rather than helping poorer farmers in the developing world, since they can't afford to pay the licences for the technology.

The developing world: subsidies remain, so developing farmers are still consistently disadvantaged in competition with farmers in the developed world. With supermarkets importing more than ever, they can sell their goods but as British farmers found before them, very much on the terms dictated by the supermarkets.

What can you do?

How you can make a mark

WHAT CAN YOU DO?

Eating well and ensuring that Britain remains an increasingly conscientious agricultural food-producing nation brings many advantages. Because food is an essential purchase, made daily or almost daily, the choices we make can have real impact, on our health, on farmers, on the communities we live in, and on the wider environment. It makes sense to eat well and make ethically sound food choices where we can. Here are some first steps:

Think about the meat you eat

Food from animals that lived a happy life may cost more but it tastes better and from a humane point of view, it has got to be the choice to make. When it comes to fish, with demand so far outstripping supply, choose fish from a sustainable source wherever possible.

First Step

Look for the organic option. If too pricey or unavailable, think about where the meat came from. Take a look at **www.meatmatters.com** to get more information on the **Quality Standard** marks.

Eat locally grown food

Eating organically grown food is important, but some scientists advise that buying locally produced foodstuffs, especially from within 12 miles of your home, is better for the environment than buying organic. It also supports local farmers in your community, giving them a better return for their products.

First Step

Use one of the many virtual farmers' markets springing up on the internet to find outlets near to you. Two good sources of information are **BigBarn, www.BigBarn.co.uk** and the **National Association of Farmers' Markets, www.farmersmarkets.net.**

Eat seasonal food: Join a box scheme

This gets fresh, in-season fruit and vegetables delivered to your door. There are many box schemes in the UK. Choose a local scheme rather than one run by a big company that might deliver across large distances. Again, this has the benefit of ensuring more of the profit goes to the farmers who have produced the goods.

First Step

Take a look at a selection of schemes approved by the **Soil Association, www.soilassociation.org.**

Buy Fairtrade

Buy Fairtrade but avoid products made by corporations who use it merely as a marketing ploy and maintain unethical business practices elsewhere.

First Step

Look for the official Fairtrade logo on produce ranging from coffee to chocolate, bananas to wine. Find out more at the **Fairtrade Foundation, www.fairtrade.org.uk.**

Avoid 'exotic' foods

Many foods such as mangoes, pineapples and grapes simply cannot be grown in the UK's mild and temperate climate, and are likely to have been imported and transported over long distances, damaging the environment through fuel emissions. Save them for special occasions.

First Step

Common sense should prevail. You can find out what food is in season at **www.eattheseasons.co.uk.** There is a useful food mile calculator available at **www.organiclinker.com/food-miles.cfm.**

Cut down on food packaging

Fresh food straight from local shops is often wrapped in biodegradable bags rather than plastic containers. Many supermarkets now use

83

recyclable packaging or sell loose.

First Step
Most supermarkets also now sell stronger "eco' **shopping bags** which are reusable and cut down on waste - use them when you shop locally or in a supermarket.

Grow your own food
If you have one, grow your own food in your garden. Smallholding is making a comeback, as people want to regain control of what they eat. If you don't have a garden, you could contact your local council and register for an allotment.

First Step
Some useful advice on "home-growing" is available at **www.organicgarden.org.uk** and **www.allotment.org.uk.**

Make your voice heard
You can lobby your MP on any matter of concern. The RSPCA takes a lead on animal welfare with its Freedom Food label. You can support farmers by how you shop, but organisations, such as the Countryside Alliance or the Women's Institute, play an active lobbying role.

First Step
Find the contact details of your local MP at **www.parliament.org.** You can also start, or join active petitions, through the Prime Minister's website at **http://petitions.pm.gov.uk.**

What can you do? / *How you can make a mark*

Further Reading

The best places to keep up-to-date

FURTHER READING

Here are some useful sources to use as a starting point for your own further reading. To keep up-to-date and have your say on food issues in the news have a look at our blog, http://blog.pocketissue.com

Keeping up-to-date
Both the BBC, www.bbc.co.uk, and The Guardian, www.guardian.co.uk, have good sections on food, health and the environment.

The National Farmers Union also has an interesting news section from a farming standpoint, www.nfuonline.com

The Policy Makers
The DEFRA website holds the latest guidelines and news, www.defra.gov.uk and includes the latest research on GM technology. For an organic viewpoint, visit the Soil Association, www.soilassocation.co.uk.

For information on Fairtrade visit www.fairtrade.org.uk.

For the latest consumer information and guidelines visit the Food Standards Agency, www.food.gov.uk.

For an international perspective, take a look at the World Trade Organisation, www.wto.org, and the European Union, http://europa.eu.

The Activists
For a rural standpoint, visit the Countryside Alliance, www.countryside-alliance.org and the Women's Institute, www.womens-institute.co.uk.

Friends of the Earth, www.foe.co.uk, and Greenpeace, www.greenpeace.org.uk, are also active campaigners on food issues.

Health and Nutrition
A guide to the basics, sponsored by some well-known brands, can be found on What's Inside Guide, www.whatsinsideguide.com.

The Glossary

Jargon-free explanations

THE GLOSSARY

Jargon-free explanations of some of the key terms and organisations.

Agribusiness

Businesses involved in the food production industry.

Antibiotic

A chemical substance derived from a mould or bacterium that kills micro organisms and cures infections.

Biodynamic

This emphasises a holistic approach to farming that excludes the use of artificial chemicals and attempts to develop an inter-relationship between plants, animals and soil.

Bird flu

Also called avian flu. Viral illness that affects birds. A current strain - H5N1 virus - is causing international concern due to the fear that it could pass from bird to humans, then between humans.

Blue tongue disease

A non-contagious disease found in sheep and cattle and spread by insects. Newly arrived in the UK in 2007.

BSE

Bovine Spongiform Encephalopathy, a disease found in cattle that can be passed to humans. Often called "mad cow" disease. There was a high-profile outbreak in the UK during the 1990s.

Common Agricultural Policy, (CAP):

Established in 1962, CAP is a system of EU agricultural subsidies and programmes that attempt to guarantee a minimum price to European farmers. Currently being amended across Europe.

Consumerism

The view that consumers, rather than producers, should control the way the economy works.

DEFRA

The department for Environment, Food and Rural Affairs regulates the farming industry in the UK.

E-coli

Bacteria found in animal intestines that can cause illness, and sometimes death, in humans.

E-numbers

Food additives that have been authorised by the European Union.

Ethylene gas

A naturally available gas used to ripen fruit and vegetables.

Factory farming

Usually livestock farming, animals are kept in confinement and in great density – see Intensive Farming below.

Fairtrade
An international trading scheme set up to ensure producers in the developing world get fair prices for their produce, and have reasonable working conditions and trading terms with the companies they supply.

Farmers' market
Markets where farmers sell their produce direct to consumers, rather than through supermarkets or high street shops.

"Fast" food
Quick and easy ready meals available from take away outlets and food retailers. Nutritional benefit varies depending upon ingredients.

Flavonoids
Naturally occurring chemical compounds most commonly known for their antioxidant activity.

FLO International
The main organisation overseeing Fairtrade production

Food miles
The number of miles food has travelled from its point of source to your plate, and the consequent damage its transport has on the environment.

Foot and mouth
A highly contagious viral disease that affects primarily cattle, pigs and sheep. Humans are very rarely affected; "very close" contact is required. The UK saw major outbreaks in 2001 and 1967.

GDA
Guideline Daily Amount. Suggested healthy daily limits for calories, fats, salt and sugar that now appear on food packaging. Often linked to the "traffic light" scheme.

GM
Genetically modified. Food containing ingredients that have had their biological characteristics modified by altering their genetic make-up.

Green Revolution
The transformation of agriculture in developing nations which led to significant increases in agricultural productivity through the spreading of intensive farming methods. The term was first used in 1968.

Herbicide
Used to kill unwanted plants, destroying specific targets while leaving the desired crop relatively unharmed.

H5N1
Strain of bird flu virus - see "bird flu" above.

Industrial farming
Another term for intensive farming.

Intensive farming

Using technological means to make animals and birds grow more quickly, prevent disease and increase land fertility and crop yields, through the use of additives, antibiotics and artificial hormones on animals, and pesticides and artificial fertilisers on crops.

"Junk" food

Food with little or no nutritional benefit with higher than average levels of fat, salt and sugars.

"Local" food

This puts the emphasis on buying food that has been produced locally, on the grounds that it is better for the environment, better nutritionally, and supports the local community.

Organic farming

Farming that avoids the use of synthetic or artificial fertilisers, pesticides and growth hormones, using instead crop rotation, animal manures and mechanical cultivation to maintain soil productivity.

Pesticide

A substance or mixture of substances intended for preventing, destroying, repelling, or lessening the damage of any pest.

"Seasonal" food

Food that can only be grown locally during a particular season e.g. in the UK, apples in early autumn or Asparagus in early summer.

Single Payment Scheme

Subsidy introduced in 2005 in the UK replacing CAP. The scheme links subsidies to land management rather than just production

"Slow" food

The slow food movement. Founded by the Italian journalist Carlo Petrini to protect endangered local foods from being extinguished by global brands. Seasonality is key.

Soil Association

The UK's leading campaigning and certification organisation for organic food and farming.

Subsidy

In agricultural terms, financial government assistance to support farmers in their work. Both the EU and US provide large subsidies to farming communities.

World Trade Organisation

International body regulating global trade tariffs, many of which affect developing farmers.

Also from Pocket Issue

Gen up on the big global issues with these essential titles from Pocket Issue... and sound knowledgeable when others don't.

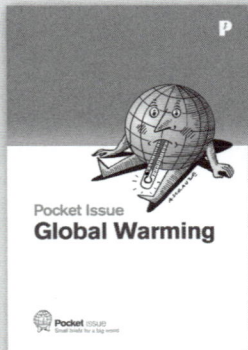

"Precisely what's needed..."
Hephzibah Anderson, The Daily Mail

"For everyone who longs to be well informed but lacks the time (or the attention span)." Alex Clark, The Observer

Order online at
www.**pocket**issue.com

Pocket issue
Small briefs for a big world